MO'
YO' MAMA!

BUST-O-PEDIA

Snap C. Pop and Kid Rank

B
BERKLEY BOOKS, NEW YORK

MO' YO' MAMA!

A Berkley Book/published by arrangement with the authors

PRINTING HISTORY
Berkley trade paperback edition / February 1996

The Penguin Putnam Inc. World Wide Web site is
http://www.penguinputnam.com

ISBN: 0-425-15214-6

PRINTED IN THE UNITED STATES OF AMERICA

15   14   13   12   11   10

To my buddy Domenick, to the Sparta family over at Poppa's Pizza, to Dave (Dave's not here), to Kathy, to Jill, and to my mama.

—Kid Rank

✳

To Johnny Boy, to The Buckster, to Debs, Andrea, Megan and all my AOL buds, and to the Kellogg's company for giving my breakfast real meaning (not).

—Snap C. Pop

✳

Grateful acknowledgment to America's Talking Television Network, WNHC, KBMS, WTLC, WFXC, WCIN, KPRS, WCKX, WMHG, WOWI, WQUE, WBLK, WUFO, KCLT, KJMS, KHRN, WLOU, WAAA, WENN, WJLD, WJBT, WTLZ, WGOK, WVOI, WOLF, WDKX, KMJJ, WWDM, WJTT, WNOO, WXOK, and WILD 107 for running the Mother's Day Yo'Mamma contests and other promotions. Thanks to the Berkley people for being so **cool**, including Lindsay Kniffen, Elizabeth Beier, and company.

✳

Special apologies to Howard Stern's mama for calling her so **ugly** that when she was born the doctor threw her away and kept the afterbirth.

✳

Special apologies to Roseanne for fully dissin' her in our first book . . . although she IS so **fat** that when she took a trip down the Grand Canyon, she got stuck.

TABLE o' CONTENTS

MOMAMAMOMAMAMOMAMAMOMAMAMOMAMAMOMAMA

v

PERSONALITY/BEHAVIOR

HYGIENE

SEXUALITY

SOCIAL STATUS

BODY PARTS

INTRODUCTION

Yo' Mama jokes were originally created over a hundred years ago. Called the "Game of Dozens" back then, and still to this day by many, the name originated from the practice of grouping "inadequate" or "damaged" slaves into groups of one dozen and selling them at bargain basement prices for the lot. To be a member of the dozens was the lowest position one could hold in the black slave community.

The Game of Dozens developed among the slave groups to provide a means of establishing and maintaining a social hierarchy, where physical violence was strictly prohibited by their

MOMAMAMOMAMAMOMAMAMOMAMAMOMAMAMOMAMAMOMAMA-

"masters." The Game of Dozens was also a form of comic relief under such harsh conditions. Given the elevated stature of Mama in the social structure of those days and the likely absence of Mama among slaves sentenced to dozens groups, disrespecting (dissin') Mama was considered the ultimate insult.

Today bustin' is not just subculture phenomena, but a mainstream form of commmunication . . . everyone's doing it, black and white, young and old, smart and stupid, fat and skinny, short and tall, clean and smelly . . . well, you get the idea. Maybe if they learned to bust in other countries, there wouldn't be any wars. Can you imagine Sadam Hussein saying to Bill Clinton, "Trade restraints? Well Yo' Mama's so stupid, she thinks Eurotrash is the waste disposal system in Belgium." And Bill responding, "Oh yeah, well Yo' Mama's so stench, you used her farts for chemical warfare against our troops." Well, thinking about it, maybe this wouldn't be such a great idea.

FOREWORD

My first brush with the Dozens ... I was about eight years old. I was attending Public School No. 7 on Kingsbridge Avenue in the Bronx, New York. It was the day that Martin Luther King Jr. was assassinated, and as usual, I was being chased by a neighborhood gang. I think the reason I was being chased was because either I was too smart not to stop or too stupid to keep running. I don't know which.

As I turned a corner into a narrow alley to escape my pursuers, I heard one of them yell out, "Yo' Mama wears combat boots," as I found my hiding spot, followed by another, who yelled, "Yeah, and Yo' Mama has a mustache, too."

Needless to say, even at the young age of eight, I wasn't at all impressed with any of those lame insults and I was getting tired of being pushed around and chased all the time. So, that day I came out of my hiding spot and confronted the leader of the gang face-to-face. I stood directly in front of him, stuck out my chest, took a deep breath and said, "I fucked Yo' Mama so many times, you should be calling me Daddy!"

After that day, I was never chased again. However, my face was black and blue for an entire week.

—Kid Rank

OFFICIAL RULES

INTRODUCTION

The Game of Dozens, like other games that have grown up on the street, have taken on some universal "unwritten" rules by which most players abide (e.g., there must be an audience; no physical contact allowed; always nonviolent). But there has never been a set of "official" rules of play that people can fall back on when there's a dispute—no way of scoring like a boxing match. We thought that it was time to change that.

The Official YMB (Yo' Mama Bust-O-Pedia) Dozens rules incorporate many of the unwritten rules of the street that have been adopted over time, in addition to offering some ideas for organized challenges, a way of scoring for advanced players, and guidelines to go by, if you choose to use them. From now on, if there's a dispute, you'll have a reference to consult to settle it.

BEFORE YOU BEGIN

Choose an emcee or referee who will set the rules (choosing from the options that follow) or restate the rules to the crowd before the match as requested by the opponents. The emcee will also watch for fouls and other calls and may play the role of judge and executioner, crowd mediator (this is a democracy), or scorekeeper if the YMB scoring system is used. It's not all work though; this is a time for an emcee to turn on the juice. He or she could even start with something like, "Ladies and gentlemen, we bring to you . . . In this corner [on this sidewalk, etc.], weighing in at . . . the champion . . . in this corner . . ." etc.

TYPES OF DOZENS GAMES

There are two ways a Dozens match can be run:

1) *Street Fight:* No set rounds or time limits. The loser eventually forfeits. These battles can be won in a matter of seconds or last for more than an hour, depending upon how evenly matched and resourceful the opponents.

2) *Three Round Competition:* Three rounds; 5 minutes of battle per round. Variation could be less or more (e.g., 2 minutes; 10 minutes) per round. First opponent to win two rounds wins this competition (i.e., if someone wins first two rounds, the game is won). This type of competition requires an emcee or referee who starts the rounds, stops them, and gets the reaction from the crowd.

COMMON CHALLENGES

There are three common types of Dozens challenges. They can be played as either a Street Fight or with the Three-Round Competition format, with or without scoring:

1) *One-on-One Challenge:* Most common challenge between two adversaries.

2) *Buddy Challenge:* Teams of two compete with one another, taking turns delivering busts.

3) *Tag-Team Challenge:* Usually teams of two against two, where each team is allowed four tag-offs (for a one-round Street Fight) or two tag-offs per five minute round (for an official Three-Round Competition).

SPECIAL CHALLENGES

There are two other special challenges with different rules for rounds and timing, and you can make up your own versions of these or invent your own:

1) *Speed Dozens:* Each individual or team has fifteen seconds to complete a bust. Game lasts for 10–15 minutes (40 to 60 busts per game). If either opponent or team goes over the 15-second limit more than three times in that game, it automatically forfeits. Therefore normal "Delay of Game" penalties do not apply here.

2) *Family Feud–Type Challenge:* Two teams of four or five battle it out with an emcee who gives out topics in 10 short rounds, and players give busts on topics in round robin fashion from one team to another.

ISSUING A CHALLENGE

There are two ways you can issue a challenge:

1) *Spontaneously Challenge:* These can happen anywhere and they do. No advance planning, just the challenge.

2) *Duel Challenge:* For the more romantic at heart, a healthy bout of Yo' Mama at sundown adds to the excitement of the fight. This is the I'll-see-you-on-the-playground-after-school type of challenge.

BEGINNING THE GAME

The emcee begins by announcing the challenge. The contest begins officially with the first Yo' Mama blow.

SCORING & WINNING

Opponents can win either by:

Popular Vote: In which spectators cheer or vote for the winner of each round. Whoever gets the loudest cheers wins. If it's a Three-Round bout, the crowd votes at least two times and a third time if the first two rounds were a tie.

Scored Vote: Similar to how it's done in boxing. Like a boxing match, if an opponent leaves the ring at any time (walks away from the challenge), he or she forfeits the game and the other opponent wins by TKO (Technical Knockout). If a match is really important and you want to score it fairly, pick one to three people (or even the whole audience if you want, but that can get a little hard to manage with a big crowd) and use the following guidelines to score that match.

Here's the official Yo' Mama Bust-O-Score system:

EVENT	POINTS
Great Bust	3
Good Bust	2
Fair Bust	1
Poor Bust	0
Already Used Bust	-1
Delay of Game (more than 30 seconds)	-2
Physical Contact (minor foul)	-5
Violent Physical Contact (illegal foul)	Forfeit

Obviously, whoever has the most points at the end—except if there's a forfeit or TKO—wins. When forfeits and TKOs happen, it's common to see rematches on another day when the opponent's wits are sharper.

TIME-OUTS

Players may elect to also have one, two, or three optional one-minute time-outs for each team in a game to get their bearings. Or each opponent or team could be given one 30-second time-out per round for each round. The emcee/referee decides this.

APPEARANCE

Yo' Mama's so fat,
she's taller when she's lying down.

Yo' Mama's so fat,
she was born on January 1st *and* 2nd.

Yo' Mama's so fat,
when she wears a yellow dress, kids try to
board her to go to school.

Yo' Mama's so fat,
every time she belches, the neighbors think
it's an earthquake.

Yo' Mama's so fat,
when I tried to drive around her to get to the
other side, I ran out of gas.

Yo' Mama's so fat,
when she tried to walk down the Grand
Canyon, she got stuck.

Yo' Mama's so fat,
she has more rolls than a bakery.

Yo' Mama's so fat,
she has to hire kids by the hour to wash her
butt cheeks.

Yo' Mama's so fat,
she looks like a parade standing still.

Yo' Mama's so fat,
when she stepped on the scale, the needle
went around so many times it screwed itself
into the floor.

Yo' Mama's so fat,
when she's walking she has to use hand
signals when she wants to turn.

Yo' Mama's so fat,
her favorite food is seconds.

Yo' Mama's so fat,
when she walks through a turnstile, she has
to make two trips.

Yo' Mama's so fat,
she trips over her own chin.

Yo' Mama's so fat,
she wipes her ass with a bedsheet.

Yo' Mama's so fat,
she's been married to your father for twenty
years and he still hasn't seen all of her.

Yo' Mama's so fat,
at her wedding, they threw puffed rice.

Yo' Mama's so fat,
as a child she could only play seek.

Yo' Mama's so fat,
her idea of exercise is lifting the food from
the plate to her mouth.

Yo' Mama's so fat,
she once boarded a ship and it became
a submarine.

Yo' Mama's so fat,

when she was born, her parents brought her home in a wheelbarrow.

Yo' Mama's so fat,

when her beeper goes off, people think she's backing up.

Yo' Mama's so fat,

people jog around her for exercise.

Yo' Mama's so fat,

she was floating in the ocean and Spain claimed her for their new world.

Yo' Mama's so fat,
when she has sex, she has to give directions.

Yo' Mama's so fat,
when she bungee jumps, she brings down
the bridge with her.

Yo' Mama's so fat,
the highway patrol made her wear a
CAUTION! WIDE TURN sign.

Yo' Mama's so fat,
she fell in love and broke it.

Yo' Mama's so fat,
whenever she goes to the beach, the tide comes in.

Yo' Mama's so fat,
she's got AMTRAK written on her leg.

Yo' Mama's so fat,
her legs are like spoiled milk—white and chunky.

Yo' Mama's so fat,
she was mistaken for God's bowling ball.

Yo' Mama's so fat,
she influences the tides.

Yo' Mama's so fat,
you have to grease the door frame and hold a
Twinkie on the other side just to get her through.

Yo' Mama's so fat,
when she goes to an all-you-can-eat buffet,
they have to install speed bumps.

Yo' Mama's so fat,
she sets off car alarms when she goes jogging.

Yo' Mama's so fat,
she put on some BVDs and by the time they
reached her waist, they spelled out
BOULEVARD.

Yo' Mama's so fat,
road workers tie a rope around her and drag her through tunnels when they want to clean them.

Yo' Mama's so fat,
the National Weather Service has to assign names to her farts.

Yo' Mama's so fat,
we went to the drive-in and didn't have to pay because we dressed her as a Chevrolet.

Yo' Mama's so fat,
she was zoned for commercial development.

Yo' Mama's so fat,
she thinks gravy is a beverage.

Yo' Mama's so fat,
she got hit by a school bus and turned
around and said, "Quit pushing."

Yo' Mama's so fat,
she crossed the sun and scientists thought it
was a solar eclipse.

Yo' Mama's so ugly,

when she was a kid and played hide and seek and it was her turn to hide, all the other kids went home.

Yo' Mama's so ugly,

no wonder you keep telling people you were adopted.

Yo' Mama's so ugly,

the last time she was on top of the Empire State Building, she was attacked by planes.

Yo' Mama's so ugly,

she's been cut out of her own baby pictures.

Yo' Mama was such an ugly child,
the stork must have had a crash landing.

Yo' Mama's so ugly,
her mother had to get drunk in order to
breast-feed her.

Yo' Mama's so ugly,
when she went to a plastic surgeon, he
wanted to add a tail.

Yo' Mama's so ugly,
her brother was an only child.

Yo' Mama's so ugly,
when she sees her therapist, he always makes
her lie on the couch facedown.

Yo' Mama's so ugly,
she's even ugly in the dark.

Yo' Mama's so ugly,
when she played in the sandbox as a child,
the cat would always bury her.

Yo' Mama has the face of a saint:
a Saint Bernard.

Yo' Mama's so ugly,
even mosquitoes refuse to bite her.

Yo' Mama's so ugly,
as a child her parents hired another kid to
play her in home movies.

Yo' Mama's so ugly,
as a child, she had to be breast-fed by the dog.

Yo' Mama's so ugly,
when all the kids were afraid of the
boogeyman, they were talkin' about yo' Mama.

Yo' Mama's so ugly,
she looks like something the cat brought in.

Yo' Mama's so ugly,
she looks like a cake that's been left out in the rain.

Yo' Mama has so many pimples,
a blind man can read her face.

Yo' Mama looks like a movie star:
Lassie.

Yo' Mama has a face like a flower:
a cauliflower.

Yo' Mama's so ugly,
when she walks into a room, the mice
jump on chairs.

Yo' Mama's so ugly,
the day she was born her father took one look at
her, then ran to the zoo and shot the stork.

**Yo' Mama's face has been lifted so
many times,**
it's out of focus.

Yo' Mama wanted to have her face lifted,
but they couldn't find a crane big enough.

Yo' Mama's so ugly,
she ought to have her face capped.

Yo' Mama's face is so ugly,
she looks like she's slept in it.

Yo' Mama's so ugly,
as a child her mother made her play in quicksand.

Yo' Mama's so ugly,
she went to the zoo and scared all the animals.

Yo' Mama's so ugly,
when she joined an ugly contest, they said,
"Sorry, no professionals."

Yo' Mama's so ugly,
when she looks out of a window she gets
arrested for mooning.

Yo' Mama's so ugly,
they filmed *Gorillas in the Mist* in her shower.

Yo' Mama's so ugly,
she makes onions cry.

Yo' Mama's so ugly,
she turned Medusa to stone.

Yo' Mama's so ugly,
the tollbooth operator gives her money to
drive through as quickly as possible.

Yo' Mama's so ugly,
the tide wouldn't even take her out.

Yo' Mama's so ugly,
they threw her away and kept the afterbirth.

Yo' Mama's so ugly,
when she was born, the doctor took her and
told her mother, "Ma'am, if this doesn't start
to cry in ten seconds, it was a tumor."

Yo' Mama's so ugly,

her mama used to put rubber bands on yo'
Mama's ears, so people would think she was
wearing a mask.

Yo' Mama's so ugly,

she couldn't get laid in a prison with a fistful
of pardons.

Yo' Mama's so ugly,

when you took her to the zoo, the zookeeper
said, "Thanks for bringing her back."

Yo' Mama's so short,
her skin drags on the floor.

Yo' Mama's so short,
I once flicked a booger at her and knocked
her out.

Yo' Mama's so short,
when she went out to dinner, I had to call the
waiter over because yo' Mama was floating
in my soup.

Yo' Mama's so short,
she could be a hood ornament.

Yo' Mama's so short,
she uses a sock as a sleeping bag.

Yo' Mama's so short,
she has to stand on her toes to go down on
a cockroach.

Yo' Mama's so short,
when it rains, she's always the last to know.

Yo' Mama's so short,
I saw her at the circus being shot out of a cap gun.

Yo' Mama's so short,
she could walk underneath a closed door.

Yo' Mama's so short,
she gets out of breath when she walks
through a shaggy rug.

Yo' Mama's so short,
she could be a refrigerator magnet.

Yo' Mama's so short,
when she pulls up her stockings, she can't see
where she's going.

Yo' Mama's so short,
she has to use a ladder to pick up a dime.

Yo' Mama's so old,
at her last birthday party, the candles cost
more than the cake.

Yo' Mama's so old,
she used to hump dinosaurs.

Yo' Mama's so old,
her idea of an exciting night in bed is
pushing the buttons on her Craftmatic
adjustable.

Yo' Mama's so old,
she counts her birthdays in Roman numerals.

Yo' Mama's so old,
she was the very first slave.

Yo' Mama's so old,
when she told me her age, I thought it was
her phone number.

Yo' Mama's so old,
she's older than your grandmother.

Yo' Mama's so old,
she has an autographed Bible.

Yo' Mama's so old,
when Cain killed Abel, she was on the jury.

Yo' Mama's so old,
that when she got divorced from her first
husband, she got the cave.

Yo' Mama's so old,
the picture on her driver's license is by
Leonardo da Vinci.

Yo' Mama's so old,
she remembers Madam Butterfly when she
was just a caterpillar.

Yo' Mama's so old,
if you ask her how she's doing, she'll paint
the answer in hieroglyphics on the wall.

Yo' Mama's so old,
she helped Moses edit down the fifteen
commandments.

Yo' Mama's so old,
she can remember a boxing match
between two white guys.

Yo' Mama looks like a million,
but nobody could be that old.

Yo' Mama's coat is so old,
the only things keeping it together are the
buttonholes.

Yo' Mama's so skinny,
when she wears a red hat, she looks like a pencil.

Yo' Mama's so skinny,
when she walks on the sidewalk, she slips through the cracks.

Yo' Mama's so skinny,
it takes two of her to make one shadow.

Yo' Mama's so skinny,
the other night when I stayed over, I accidentally brushed my teeth with her.

Yo' Mama's so skinny,
when she walks into a pool room, she gets chalked.

Yo' Mama's so skinny,
when she wears a black dress, she looks like a closed umbrella.

Yo' Mama's so skinny,
she had to be X-rayed for meat.

Yo' Mama's so skinny,
she hula hoops with a rubberband.

Yo' Mama's so skinny,
her shadow weighs more than she does.

Yo' Mama's so skinny,
she could model for thermometers.

Yo' Mama's so skinny,
she once bought a necktie and made a dress
out of it.

Yo' Mama's so tall,
when she drops something on her toe, she
doesn't scream until the next day.

Yo' Mama's so tall,
when a plane passes by, she knows what
they're serving for dinner.

Yo' Mama's so tall,
she tripped in Michigan and hit her head in
Florida.

Yo' Mama's so black,
when she walks outside at night, she's invisible.

Yo' Mama's so black,
when she spits, Bosco comes out.

Yo' Mama's so black,
when she stands next to my car, I think
somebody stole it.

Yo' Mama's so black,
when she stands next to a wall, you think
she's an entrance.

Yo' Mama's so white,
when she's in the kitchen, you think she's the
refrigerator.

Yo' Mama's so white,
she shops at KKKmart.

Yo' Mama's so white,
when she goes out, all the kids scream,
"Hey, Good Humor man!"

Yo' Mama's so white,
she could make the dirtiest neighborhood
look clean just by walking in it.

INTELLIGENCE

Yo' Mama's so dumb,
she thinks a boycott is a male bed.

Yo' Mama's so dumb,
she doesn't use toothpaste because her teeth
aren't loose.

Yo' Mama's so stupid,
she tried to counterfeit a one-dollar bill by
erasing the zero from a ten.

Yo' Mama's so stupid,
she has a hard time writing the number 11
because she can't figure out which number
comes first.

Yo' Mama's so stupid,
she won a gold medal in a one hundred-yard
dash then went and had it bronzed.

Yo' Mama's so stupid,
she has a twin sister but keeps forgetting her
birthday.

Yo' Mama's so stupid,
last week somebody stole her car, but she's not
worried since she got the license plate number.

Yo' Mama's so stupid,
she thinks intercourse is the time off between
classes at school.

Yo' Mama's so stupid,
I once said to her, "There's a dead bird."
She looked up.

Yo' Mama's so dumb,
she has her address tattooed to her forehead,
so if she gets lost, she can mail herself home.

Yo' Mama's so dumb,
she has to take her blouse off to count to two.

Yo' Mama's so stupid,
if you gave her a penny for her thoughts,
you'd have change coming.

Yo' Mama's so dumb,
if you want her to spell Mississippi, she'd ask,
"The river or the state?"

Yo' Mama's so dumb and dyslexic,
she told me she's an atheist—she doesn't
believe in dog.

Do you know what "gross stupidity" is?
One hundred forty-four of yo' Mamas.

Yo' Mama's so stupid,
she works as a bank teller. Last week I came in and asked her to check my balance, so she knocked me down.

Yo' Mama's so dumb,
she has brain damage—a piece of paper fell on her head.

Yo' Mama's so stupid,
she puts blush on her head when she makes up her mind.

Yo' Mama's so stupid,
she had to take the I.Q. test twice in order to
get it up to a whole number.

Ha

Yo' Mama's so stupid,
she thinks Dr. Spock is a Vulcan.

Yo' Mama ought to blow her brains out,
she's got nothing to lose.

Yo' Mama's so stupid,
she always thinks twice before saying
nothing.

Yo' Mama had an operation on her butt—
the doctor removed her brain.

Yo' Mama's so stupid,
she thinks Bugs Bunny is a good actor.

Yo' Mama's so stupid,
she thinks the First Lady is Eve.

Yo' Mama's so stupid,
her idea of safe sex is locking the car door.

Yo' Mama's so stupid,
she lost her job as an elevator operator
because she kept forgetting the route.

Yo' Mama's so stupid,
the stork that delivered her should have been
arrested for smuggling dope.

Yo' Mama's so dumb,
she thinks a can opener is a key to the john.

Yo' Mama's so dumb,
she takes the screens off the windows to let
the flies out.

Yo' Mama's so stupid,
she squeezed a can of soup to see if it was fresh.

Yo' Mama's so dumb,
she spent an entire day in a revolving door
looking for a doorknob.

Yo' Mama's so stupid,
she thinks cornflakes is a foot disease.

Yo' Mama's so stupid,
she plays cards with gloves on so nobody
can see her hand.

Yo' Mama's so stupid,
she smiles and says "cheese" for X ray pictures.

Yo' Mama's so stupid,
when she loses a button on her blouse, she
sews up the buttonhole.

Yo' Mama's so stupid,
she asked you, "What is the number for 9-1-1?"

Yo' Mama's so stupid,
she thought gangrene was a golf course
for derelicts.

Yo' Mama's so stupid,
on her job application under "Education,"
she put "Hooked on Phonics."

Yo' Mama's so stupid,
on her tax return where it said "Sign Here,"
she wrote "Scorpio."

Yo' Mama's so stupid,
when she tried to commit suicide, she
jumped out the basement window.

Yo' Mama's so stupid,
when she tried to breast-feed, she burned her
nipples in the boiling water.

Yo' Mama's so stupid,
she's still watching *The Neverending Story*.

Yo' Mama's so stupid,
when the gynecologist asked her to describe
her flow, she said, "My flo's linoleum!"

Yo' Mama's so stupid,
the first time she used a vibrator, she cracked
her front teeth.

Yo' Mama's so stupid,
when she asked you what jeans you were
wearing and you said, "Guess," she said, "I
don't know, Levi's?"

Yo' Mama's so stupid,
she applied for UNCF and they rejected her,
telling her, "Your mind is worth wasting."

Yo' Mama's so stupid,
she thinks a protein is someone in favor of
young people.

Yo' Mama's so stupid,
she once got amnesia and became smarter.

Yo' Mama's so stupid,
when she took you to the airport and saw a
sign that said AIRPORT LEFT, she turned around
and went home.

Yo' Mama's so stupid,
she thinks an artery is someone who studies fine art.

Yo' Mama's so stupid,
she thinks St. Ives is a church.

Yo' Mama's so stupid,
she didn't see *Malcolm X* because she never saw
the first nine.

PERSONALITY/ BEHAVIOR

Yo' Mama's so boring,
her idea of an exciting evening is raising the
temperature on the electric blanket.

Yo' Mama's so boring,
she once woke up from a nap and found a tag
on her toe.

Yo' Mama's so boring,
she once tried computer dating, and they
matched her up with rice cakes.

Yo' Mama's so boring,
if she went on TV, she'd come out in black
and white.

Yo' Mama's so boring,
I've seen letter openers sharper than her.

Yo' Mama's so tough,
she flosses with barbed wire.

Yo' Mama's so tough,
she washes her face with Brillo.

Yo'Mama's so tough,
she'd eat the boogers out of a dead man's nose.

Yo' Mama's so tough,
when she was born and the doctor slapped
her bottom, yo' Mama shot him.

Yo' Mama's so tough,
I've seen her kill two birds with one stone.

Yo' Mama's so nasty,
she could clip a hedge with her tongue.

Yo' Mama's so nasty,
her shadow won't keep her company.

Yo' Mama's so temperamental:
ninety percent temper and ten percent mental.

Yo' Mama's so nasty,
she once threw an anchor to a drowning man.

Yo' Mama's so nasty,
when she wants your opinion, she'll give it to you.

Yo' Mama's so nasty,
she wears a bone through her nose from
your younger brother's left arm.

Yo' Mama's tongue is so sharp,
she cut her own throat.

Yo' Mama's so nasty,
she sends get-well cards to hypochondriacs.

Yo' Mama's such a loser,
they call her Toilet Paper, cause she's shit on
by everyone.

Yo' Mama's such a loser,
she has to rent a shadow.

Yo' Mama's such a loser,
she once put a seashell to her ear and got a
busy signal.

Yo' Mama's such a loser,
they edited her out of her own wedding video.

Yo' Mama's such a loser,
she sent her picture to the Lonely Hearts Club,
and they replied, "We're not that lonely."

Yo' Mama's such a loser,
she's the lifeguard at a car wash.

Yo' Mama's such a loser,
she has cavities in her false teeth.

Yo' Mama's so cheap,
she told yo' baby sister Santa died.

Yo' Mama's so cheap,
she installed a pay toilet in the guest room.

Yo' Mama's so cheap,
friends have to call her on a 1-900 line.

Yo' Mama's so cheap,
she charged admission to your family's
Thanksgiving dinner.

Yo' Mama's so cheap,
she exchanges dogs at the animal shelter as
soon as they get hungry.

Yo' Mama's so cheap,
when she took your kid brother to the
movies and he asked for popcorn, yo' Mama
told him to check the floor.

Yo' Mama's so cheap,
she saw an advertisement for funerals at half
price, so she committed suicide.

Yo' Mama's so cheap,

when she saw the Sally Struthers ad that says you could support a child in India for only thirty-two cents a day, she decided to send you there.

Yo' Mama's so cheap,

she once squeezed a penny so hard, she gave Lincoln a black eye.

Yo' Mama's so lazy,
the city just made her a landmark.

Yo' Mama's so lazy,
she fell asleep during a nap.

Yo' Mama's so lazy,
she rides the revolving door on other
people's pushes.

Yo' Mama's so lazy,
she bought the audio cassette version of
Where's Waldo.

Yo' Mama's so lazy,
she bought the new Kathy Smith aerobics video, then laid down on the couch to watch it.

Yo' Mama's so lazy,
she tried to rob a bank by faxing her hold-up note.

Yo' Mama's so lazy,
she hires people to exercise for her.

Yo' Mama's so lazy,
when she gets pissed off at someone, she gives them only half the finger.

Yo' Mama's so senile,
she meets new and fascinating people every
day — in her own family.

Yo' Mama's so senile,
you and your sister have to wear name tags
around the house.

Yo' Mama's so senile,
yesterday she cut herself and forgot to bleed.

Yo' Mama's so senile,
at her last birthday, she lit a match to see if
she'd finished blowing out all the candles.

Yo' Mama's such a drunk,
she never drinks unless she's alone or with someone.

Yo' Mama never drinks and drives,
she might hit a bump and spill her drink.

Yo' Mama's such a drunk,
if it weren't for the olives in the martinis, she'd probably starve to death.

Yo' Mama's such a drunk,
one day she saw a sign that said DRINK CANADA DRY!, so she went to Canada.

Yo' Mama's such a bad driver,
she has a bumper sticker that says: IF YOU
DON'T LIKE HOW I DRIVE, STAY OFF THE SIDEWALK.

Yo' Mama's such a bad driver,
she drives fifty-five miles per fender.

Yo' Mama's such a bad driver,
anyone driving faster than her is an Idiot, and
anyone driving slower than her is an Asshole.

Yo' Mama gets pulled over so much,
the cops issued her season tickets.

Yo' Mama's such a chain smoker,
Marlboro installed a machine in her house.

Yo' Mama's such a chain smoker,
she's read many books on the harmful effects
of smoking, so she decided to give up reading.

Yo' Mama's such a chain smoker,
she listened to an audiocassette on how to
quit smoking. It was so relaxing that she lit
up a pack while she listened.

Yo' Mama's such a chain smoker,
it was suggested by her doctor to only smoke
after sex ... now she's up to five packs per day.

HYGIENE

Yo' Mama's so stench,
when you drive by her house, you think
you're in Elizabeth, New Jersey.

Yo' Mama's so stench,
she should have been a bombardier, cause
when she sits on the toilet, she drops some
powerful bombs.

Yo' Mama's so stench,
neighborhood cats keep following her around.

Yo' Mama's so stench,
I guess she really is full of shit.

Yo' Mama's so stench,
hound dogs refuse to track her down.

Yo' Mama's so stench,
she throws a pair of her used underwear in the closet to save on mothballs.

Yo' Mama's breath is so bad,
she rinses with Lysol.

Yo' Mama's breath is so bad,
when she yawns, her teeth duck.

Yo' Mama's so stench,
her shit is glad to escape.

Yo' Mama's so stench,
she put on Secret deodorant and it told
on her.

Yo' Mama's so dirty,
her crabs have crabs.

Yo' Mama never uses her shower,
she doesn't want to get any dirt in it.

Yo' Mama's so dirty,
the other day she took a shower and turned
white.

Yo' Mama's so dirty,
she uses Raid as deodorant.

SEXUALITY

Yo' Mama's so loose,
she's pregnant again—but this time she decided to name the baby after the father . . .
NAVY!

Yo' Mama's like a buffet,
you help yourself.

Yo' Mama's so loose,
she's been boarded more times than Amtrack.

Yo' Mama's so loose,
she has landing lights on her stomach.

Yo' Mama wears kneepads,
'cause she goes down all the time.

Yo' Mama's like a doorknob,
everybody gets a turn.

Yo' Mama never screws strangers,
she always asks their name first.

Yo' Mama's like an elephant,
she rolls on her back for peanuts.

Yo' Mama's so loose,
she was thirty-two when she found out cars
had front seats.

Yo' Mama's like a napkin—
she's always on someone's lap.

Yo' Mama's such a ho',
she has a sign on her bed that reads:
GROUP RATES.

Yo' Mama's so loose,
the other night when I was going down on her, I looked inside and saw another guy smiling and smoking a cigarette.

Yo' Mama's such a ho',
she keeps a change-maker in her pantyhose.

Yo' Mama's worked the streets so long,
they made her an honorary streetlight.

Yo' Mama's such a slut,
when she had sex education in high school, *she* was the homework.

Yo' Mama's like a nail,
she loves to get hammered.

Yo' Mama's like a screen door—
after a couple of bangs, she tends to loosen up.

Yo' Mama's like the Pillsbury doughboy—
everyone gets a poke.

If Yo' Mama had as many pricks
sticking out of her as she has had in her,
she'd look like a porcupine.

SOCIAL STATUS

Yo' Mama's so poor,
homeless people give her money for food.

Yo' Mama's so poor,
last week she had a party and served the
guests paint chips.

Yo' Mama's so poor,
the roaches moved out.

Yo' Mama's so poor,
she has to wind up her television.

Yo' Mama's so poor,
when she goes to the park, the pigeons feed her.

Yo' Mama's so poor,
she tells stories about the time she almost ate
at a restaurant.

Yo' Mama's so poor,
the dog eats at the house next door.

Yo' Mama's so poor,
her zip code has only one number.

Yo' Mama's so poor,
the tooth fairy leaves her IOUs.

Yo' Mama's so poor,
an orphan child from Bangladesh supports her.

Yo' Mama's so poor,
everybody got a change of underwear for
Christmas—you changed with yo' brother
and yo' Mama changed with yo' sister.

Yo' Mama's so poor,
on your birthday, she gave you a picture of a birthday cake.

Yo' Mama's so poor,
last week a mugger gave her money.

Yo' Mama's so poor,
she had to paint the house before they could condemn it.

Yo' Mama's so poor,
she can't afford shoes so she laces up her feet.

Yo' Mama's so poor,
she can't even afford to go window shopping.

Yo' Mama's so poor,
the other day I saw her on the street rolling a
trash can. When I asked her what she was
doing, she said, "Redecorating."

Yo' Mama's so poor,
your family ate cereal with a fork to save milk.

Yo' Mama's so poor,
she was in Kmart with a box of Hefty bags.
I said, "What are you doing?"
She said, "Buying luggage."

Yo' Mama's neighborhood is so bad,
anyone not missing a body part is considered
a sissy.

Yo' Mama's neighborhood is so bad,
the supermarket has pictures of missing cops
on the back of milk cartons.

Yo' Mama's neighborhood is so bad,
the gun store ran a back-to-school special on Uzis.

Yo' Mama's neighborhood is so bad,
kids trick-or-treat for nose candy.

Yo' Mama's neighborhood is so bad,
the roaches wear bulletproof vests.

Yo' Mama's neighborhood is so bad,
the most popular song on the street is the
police siren.

Yo' Mama's neighborhood is so bad,
the most popular form of transportation is
the ambulance.

Yo' Mama's house is so small,
I've seen doghouses bigger than that.

Yo' Mama's house is so small,
when you go to the toilet, you have to shit
standing up.

Yo' Mama's house is so small,
the kitchen and bathroom are in the same
room, so you can eat and shit at
the same time.

Yo' Mama's house is so dirty,
cockroaches have to crawl around in
combat boots.

Yo' Mama's house is so dirty,
the city just declared it their new dump site.

Yo' Mama's house is so small,
the mice walk around hunchback.

Yo' Mama's house is so small,
she once enlarged it by scraping off
the wallpaper.

BODY PARTS

Yo' Mama's butt is so big,
when she runs, it looks like Fat Albert stuck
in a potato sack.

Yo' Mama's butt is so big,
it has its own heart and lungs.

Yo' Mama's bald,
but she still has dandruff.

Yo' Mama's so bald,
she buys imitation dandruff whenever she
wears a wig.

Yo' Mama's so bald,
it looks like her neck is blowing bubblegum.

Yo' Mama's so bald,
I can see myself and don't I look good.

Yo' Mama's so bald,
her head slips off the pillow when she sleeps.

Yo' Mama's so bald,
when she dreams at night, it's projected on
the walls.

Yo' Mama's so bald,
when she puts on a turtleneck, her head
looks like a roll-on deodorant stick.

Yo' Mama's so hairy,
her knees have bangs.

Yo' Mama's so hairy,
she looks like all three members of ZZ Top.

Yo' Mama's so hairy,

when she wraps her arms around your father,
he looks like he's wearing a fur coat.

Yo' Mama's so hairy,

she looks like a giant used Brillo pad.

Yo' Mama's so hairy,

she has something that most men want—a beard.

Yo' Mama's so hairy,

she's got Afros on her nipples.

Yo' Mama's so hairy,

Bigfoot is taking *her* picture.

Yo' Mama's nose is so big,

she once sheltered two homeless people with it for an entire month.

Yo' Mama's nose is so big,

she once sneezed so hard, a nearby plane flew off course.

Yo' Mama's nose is so big,

when God gave out noses, yo' Mama thought he said roses, so she ordered a big red one.

Yo' Mama's nose is so big,
she was the best act in the circus—she shot
two midgets out of it at the same time.

Yo' Mama's nose is so big,
when she inhales, the house gets clean.

Yo' Mama's feet are so big,
when she walks through the streets at night,
she has to put flood lights on them.

Yo' Mama's ears are so big,
she looks like Ross Perot.

Yo' Mama's ears are so big,
she can talk dirty to herself.

Yo' Mama's ears are so big,
she looks like a car with both doors open.

Yo' Mama's ears are so big,
she could model for Ping-Pong paddles.

Yo' Mama's ears are so big,
she can hear conversations between God and
other people.

Yo' Mama's missing so many teeth,
when she opens her mouth it looks like
a graveyard.

Yo' Mama's teeth are so yellow,
when she smiles, cars slow down.

Yo' Mama's teeth are so bad,
I've seen better teeth on a comb.

Yo' Mama's teeth are so bad,
she's the original model for the
jack-o'-lantern.

Yo' Mama's teeth are so rotten,
when she smiles, they look like dice.

Yo' Mama's got so many teeth missing,
it looks like her tongue is in jail.

Yo' Mama's mouth is so big,
when she's on the beach with friends, her
tongue gets sunburnt.

Yo' Mama's mouth is so big,
she could play the saxophone from
both ends.

Yo' Mama's so cross-eyed,
she has to walk sideways.

Yo' Mama's so cross-eyed,
when she opens her right eye, all she can see
is her left eye.

Yo' Mama's so cross-eyed,
she'd put your baby sister on the table, then
powder the kid next door.

Yo' Mama's glasses are so thick,
when she looks at the ground, she sets insects
on fire.

Yo' Mama's so cross-eyed,
I could stand in front of her and she wouldn't
see me.

Yo' Mama's so cross-eyed,
when she cries, the tears from her right eye
fall down her left cheek.

Yo' Mama's so cross-eyed,
she kisses the cat good night and puts your
father out.

Yo' Mama's so cross-eyed,
she could watch a tennis match without
moving her head.

Yo' Mama's so bowlegged,
you could hang her on the wall for
good luck.

Yo' Mama's so bowlegged,
she looks like two giraffes kissing.

Yo' Mama's so bowlegged,
the football team wants to use her
as a goalpost.

Yo' Mama's so bowlegged,
she could get out of a car from both sides at
the same time.

Yo' Mama's tits are so big,
if she put wigs on them, she'd look like
Siamese triplets.

Yo' Mama's tits are so big,
they had to take the windshield off the car.

Yo' Mama's tits are so big,
she has to back up to ring a doorbell.

Yo' Mama's measurements are 83-62-85,
and her other breast is even bigger.

Yo' Mama's tits are so big,
when your father has sex with her, he thinks
he's with three women.

Yo' Mama's tits are so small,
she carries her nipples in her pocket.

Yo' Mama's tits are so small,
she has to hold up her bra with suspenders.

Yo' Mama's so flat,
yo' brother uses her as a surfboard.

Yo' Mama's so flat,
she's the only woman in the entire world
with two backs.

Yo' Mama's so flat,
carpenters use her as a level.

Yo' Mama's so flat,
she got a job at a hardware store modeling walls.

Yo' Mama's so flat,
when you were a baby, you had to nurse through a straw.

READER BUSTS
Our Winners

There are a lot of creative people out there and the reader mail we got proved it. Here are the winners of our Yo' Mama Bust Invitational. Thanks to everyone else for their submissions!

Yo' Mama's so stupid,
she thinks Shaq is a run-down house.
—Lin-Z Arakelian (Stamford, CT)

Yo' Mama's so fat,
the National Law Enforcement Agency made her wear a sign on her butt saying: CRACK KILLS.
—Volena Howe (Rochester, NY)

Yo' Mama's so stupid,
she thinks virgin wool comes from a lamb
that's never been laid.
—George Bentson (Paterson, NJ)

Yo' Mama's so hairy,
Bigfoot took pictures of her.
—David Torrence (Tarzana, CA)

Yo' Mama's so ugly,
she runs with the pack.
—Lydia Toth (Sunnyvale, CA)

Yo' Mama's so ugly,
the Red Cross talked her out of being an organ donor.
—Mike Donovan (Spokane, WA)

Yo' Mama's so stupid,

if her brains were dynamite, she wouldn't have enough to blow her nose!
—Geraldine Desimon, 73-year-old mama (Kent, WA)

Yo' Mama's so old,

Miss Daisy drives her!
—Dylan Kinney (Muncie, IN)

Yo' Mama's so fat,

when the circus comes to town, they think she's the tent!
—Beth Ann Lynch (Penfield, NY)

Yo' Mama's so old,
she has flashbacks of the big bang!

—P. J. Knoetgen (*Avalon, NJ*)

Yo' Mama's such a ho',
not only did she go down in history; she went down on history.

—Monica Larina (Brooklyn, NY)

Yo' Mama's so fat,
in her class photo, she was the front row!

—Daniel Woods (Grovetown, GA)

Yo' Mama's so poor,
she hangs the toilet paper out to dry.*

Yo' Mama's so stupid,
she thinks dreadlocks are some new
antitheft device.*

Yo' Mama's like a police station,
dicks go in and out all day long.*

Yo' Mama and I are into rock 'n roll,
she tries to rock my world and then I roll her
off the bed.
—Louis Rosen (Miami, FL)*

SPECIAL ACKNOWLEDGMENT

The authors wish to acknowledge the winning bust of the Wild 107 FM Mother's Day Yo' Mama Contest, judged live on the air by Kid Rank May 12, 1995. Over 25 entries were received, but only one could be the winner:

Yo' Mama's so stupid,
she flunked kindergarten because she didn't know how to scribble.

Our congratulations to Kathy of San Francisco.

YO! WE'LL MAKE YOU FAMOUS ONCE MORE!

Yo' Own Yo' Mama Submission Form

Andy Warhol once said that everyone is famous for at least 15 minutes in their lifetime. Here's yo' big chance at fame! Use the form on the next page to send us your *original* Yo' Mamas. If we use it in our next book, we'll put your name by it and you'll go down in history. *And*, we'll send you a free copy of our next book if we use it. So don't hesitate!

MOMAMAMOMAMAMOMAM**119**MAMAMOMAMAMOMAMA-

Cut here or copy this information on an 8-1/2" x 11" piece of paper.

Name: _____

Address: _____

Bust: _____

_____

_____

Send to: Mo' Yo' Mama, P.O. Box 127, Stony Point, NY 10980

I hereby declare that the above quote ("Quote") is of my own original author-ship and agree to allow the authors of Mo' Yo' Mama to use it in any upcoming book and/or for any other purpose that they see fit at their discre-tion, as long as the authors identify its source as myself if published.

Print Name: _____ Date: _____

Signature (if 18 years or older) _____

Parent or Guardian Name (if under 18 years) _____

Parent or Guardian Signature (if under 18 years) _____

_____